GREAT.

ANTHOLOG

GREAT HORSES AND GALLANT HORSEMEN

GREAT HORSES AND GALLANT HORSEMEN

Inspiring poems collected by
MARY VAUGHAN
and illustrated by
JOHN KING

Quiller Press
London

First published 1988 by Quiller Press Limited
46 Lillie Rd, London SW6 1PN

Copyright © Compilation and Mary Vaughan poems, Mary Vaughan 1988

Copyright © Illustrations John King 1988

ISBN 1 870948 11 4

20/10/89

Design and production in association with Book Production Consultants, 47 Norfolk Street, Cambridge.

Typeset by Witwell Ltd, Southport

Printed and bound by Billings, Worcester

CONTENTS

The Author's parents, owner and master of the CCH Hunt.

Hunt button of the CCH.

FOREWORD

In making this collection of sporting poetry, which I hope may delight the young who may not know them all, and the not-so-young who may well have forgotten them, I am activated by the desire that these stirring poems should not be lost to posterity.

For hundreds of years horses and hounds, hunting and racing, have made an important contribution to the British way of life and to the British character.

Love of the Chase, admiration of great horses and feats of jockeyship still stir the blood even in this industrial and mechanized age.

Poetry is a form of building with words, making vivid pictures in the mind which can convey the excitement, drama, and courage of different situations. The magic of a hunting morning, thrilling 'Gone Away' of the huntsman's horn, music of hounds speaking the line; high courage of bold horses battling out great races, and the bravery of jockeys who ride all sorts of mounts in all sorts of weather; and our humbler equine friends, all find their place in these poems, some of which I learnt as a child from my mother (one of the greatest horsewomen in Ireland) and others gathered on my way through life, but all loved and valued by me. It is my hope that they may strike a chord in other hearts where today there are so many young people involved in Pony Clubs, Hunter Trials, Eventing, Riding for the Disabled – which Princess Anne is President of – and, though hunting has inevitably changed, I am told that there are more packs of hounds and more people hunting than ever.

I would like to thank John King for his illustrations and Barbara Margerison for typing the manuscripts.

Mary Vaughe

AT GALWAY RACES

There where the course is,
Delight makes all of the one mind,
The riders upon the galloping horses,
The crowd that closes in behind:
We, too, had good attendance once,
Hearers and hearteners of the work;
Aye, horsemen for companions,
Before the merchant and the clerk
Breathed on the world with timid breath.
Sing on: somewhere at some new moon,
We'll learn that sleeping is not death,
Hearing the whole earth change its tune,
Its flesh being wild, and it again
Crying aloud as the racecourse is,
And we find heartners among men
That ride upon horses.

W. B. Yeats

THE CLIPPER THAT STANDS IN THE STALL AT THE TOP

Go strip him, lad! Now, sir, I think you'll declare
Such a picture you never set eyes on before.
He was bought in at Tatt's for three hundred I swear,
And he's worth all the money to look at, and more;
For the pick of the basket, the show of the shop,
Is the Clipper that stands in the stall at the top.

In the records of racing I read their career,
There were none of the sort but could gallop and stay,
At Newmarket his sire was the best of his year,
And the Yorkshiremen boast of his dam to this day;
But never a likelier foal did she drop,
Than this Clipper that stands in the stall at the top.

A head like a snake, and a skin like a mouse,
An eye like a woman, bright, gentle, and brown,
With loins and a back that would carry a house,
And quarters to lift him smack over a town!
What's a leap to the rest, is to him but a hop,
This Clipper that stands in the stall at the top.

When the country is deepest, I give you my word,
'Tis a pride and a pleasure to put him along,
O'er fallow and pasture he sweeps like a bird,
And there's nothing too wide, nor too high, nor too strong;
For the ploughs cannot choke, nor the fences can crop,
This Clipper that stands in the stall at the top.

Last Monday we ran for an hour in the Vale,
Not a bullfinch was trimmed, of a gap not a sign!
All the ditches were double, each fence had a rail;
And the farmers had locked every gate in the line,
So I gave him the office, and over them – Pop!
Went the Clipper that stands in the stall at the top.

I'd a lead of them all when we came to the brook,
A big one – a bumper – and up to your chin.
As he threw it behind him, I turned for a look,
There were eight of us had it, and seven got in!
Then he shook his lean head when he heard them go plop!
This Clipper stands in the stall at the top.

Ere we got to the finish, I counted but few,
And never a coat without dirt, but my own.
To the good horse I rode, all the credit was due,
When the others were tiring, he scarcely was blown;
For the best of the pace is unable to stop
The Clipper that stands in the stall at the top.

You may put on his clothes – every sportsman, they say,
In his lifetime has one that outrivals the rest,
So the pearl of my casket I've shown you today
The gentlest, the gamest – the boldest, the best –
And I never will part, by a sale or a swop,
With my Clipper that stands in the stall at the top!

G. J. Whyte-Melville

THE GALLOPING SQUIRE

Come, I'll show you a country that none can surpass,
For a flyer to cross like a bird on the wing,
We have acres of woodland and oceans of grass,
We have game in the autumn and cubs in the spring,
We have scores of good fellows hang out in the shire,
But the best of them all is the Galloping Squire.

The Galloping Squire to the saddle has got,
While the dewdrop is melting in gems on the thorn,
From the kennel he's drafted the pick of his lot,
How they swarm to his cheer! How they fly to his horn!
Like harriers turning or chasing like fire,
"I can trust 'em, each hound!" says the Galloping Squire.

One wave of his arm to the covert they throng,
'Yoi! wind him! and rouse him! By jove! he's away!"
Through a gap in the oaks see them speeding along,
O'er the open like pigeons, "they mean it today!
You may jump till you're sick – you may spur till you tire!
For it's catch 'em who can!" says the Galloping Squire

Then he takes the old horse by the head, and he sails,
In the wake of his darlings, all ear and all eye,
As they come in his line, o'er banks, fences, and rails,
The cramped ones to creep, and the fair ones to fly.
It's a very queer place that will put in the mire,
Such a rare one to ride as the Galloping Squire.

But a fallow has brought to their noses the pack,
And the pasture beyond is with cattle-stains spread,
One wave of his arm, and the Squire, in a crack,
Has lifted and thrown in his beauties at head.
"On a morning like this, it's small help you require,
But he's forward, I'll swear!" says the Galloping Squire.

So forty fair minutes they run and they race,
'Tis a Heaven to some! 'tis a lifetime to all,
Though the horses we ride are such gluttons for pace,
There are stout ones that stop, there are safe ones that fall.
But the names of the vanquished need never transpire,
For they're all at the rear of the Galloping Squire.

Till the gamest old varmint that ever drew breath,
All stiffened and draggled, held high for a throw,
O'er the squire's jolly visage, is grinning in death,
Ere he dashes him down to be eaten below,
While the daws flutter out from a neighbouring spire
At the thrilling who-whoop of the Galloping Squire.

And the labourer at work, and the lord in his hall,
Have a jest or a smile when they hear of the sport,
In ale or in claret he's toasted by all,
For they never expect to see more of the sort.
And long may it be ere he's forced to retire,
For we breed very few like the Galloping Squire.

G. J. Whyte-Melville

The Leap Of Roushan Beg

Mounted on Kyrat strong and fleet,
His chestnut steed with four white feet,
Roushan Beg, called Kurroglou,
Son of the road and bandit chief,
Seeking refuge and relief,
Up the mountain pathway flew.

Such was Kyrat's wondrous speed,
Never yet could any steed
Reach the dust-cloud in his course.
More than maiden, more than wife,
More than gold and next to life
Roushan the Robber loved his horse.

In the land that lies beyond
Erzeroum and Trebizond,
Garden-girt his fortress stood;
Plundered khan, or caravan
Journeying north from Koordistan,
Gave him wealth and wine and food.

Seven hundred and fourscore
Men at arms his livery wore,
Did his bidding night and day.
Now, through regions all unknown,
He was wandering, lost, alone,
Seeking without guide his way.

Suddenly the pathway ends,
Sheer the precipice descends,
Loud the torrent roars unseen;
Thirty feet from side to side
Yawns the chasm; on air must ride
He who crosses this ravine.

Following close in his pursuit,
At the precipice's foot,
Reyhan the Arab of Orfah
Halted with his hundred men,
Shouting upward from the glen,
'La Illah illa Allah!'

Gently Roushan Beg caressed
Kyrat's forehead, neck and breast;
Kissed him upon both his eyes;
Sang to him in his wild way,
As upon the topmost spray
Sings a bird before it flies.

'O my Kyrat, O my steed,
Round and slender as a reed,
Carry me this peril through!
Satin housing shall be thine,
Shoes of gold, O Kyrat mine,
O thou soul of Kurroglou!

'Soft thy skin as silken skein,
Soft as woman's hair thy mane,
Tender are thine eyes and true;
All thy hoofs like ivory shine,
Polished bright; O, life of mine,
Leap, and rescue Kurroglou!'

Kyrat, then, the strong and fleet,
Drew together his four white feet,
Paused a moment on the verge,
Measured with his eye the space,
And into the air's embrace
Leaped as leaps the ocean surge.

As the ocean surge o'er sand
Bears a swimmer safe to land,
Kyrat safe his rider bore;
Rattling down the deep abyss
Fragments of the precipice
Rolled like pebbles on a shore.

Roushan's tasselled cap of red
Trembled not upon his head,
Careless sat he and upright;
Neither hand nor bridle shook,
Nor his head he turned to look,
As he galloped out of sight.

Flash of harness in the air,
Seen a moment like the glare
Of a sword drawn from its sheath;
Thus the phantom horseman passed,
And the shadow that he cast
Leaped the cataract underneath.

Reyhan the Arab held his breath
While the vision of life and death
Passed above him. 'Allahu!'
Cried he. 'In all Koordistan
Lives there not so brave a man
As this Robber Kurroglou!'

Longfellow

The Lord Of The Valley

Hunters are fretting, and hacks in a lather,
Sportsmen arriving from left and from right;
Bridle-roads bringing them, see how they gather,
Dotting the meadows in scarlet and white.
Foot-people staring and horsemen preparing,
Now there's a murmur, a stir, and a shout,
Fresh from his carriage, as bridegroom in marriage,
The Lord of the Valley leaps gallantly out.

Time, the avenger, neglecting or scorning,
Gazes about him in beauteous disdain,
Lingers to toy with the whisper of morning,
Daintily, airily, paces the plain.
Then in a second, his course having reckoned,
Line that all Leicestershire cannot surpass,
Fleet as the swallow, when summer-winds follow,
The Lord of the Valley skims over the grass

Where shall we take him? Ah! now for the tussle,
These are the beauties, can stoop, and can fly,
Down go their noses, together they bustle,
Dashing and flinging, and scorning to cry.
Never stand dreaming, while yonder they're streaming,
If ever you meant it, man, mean it today!
Bold ones are riding and fast ones are striding,
The Lord of the Valley is forward, away!

Hard on his track o'er the open, and facing
The cream of the country, the pick of the chase,
Mute as a dream, his pursuers are racing,
Silence, you know's the criterion of pace.
Swarming and driving, while man and horse striving,
By hugging and cramming scarce live with them still,
The fastest are failing, the truest are tailing,
The Lord of the Valley is over the Hill!

Yonder a steed is rolled up with his master,
Here, in a double, another lies cast;
Faster and faster come grief and disaster,
All but the good ones are weeded at last.
Hunters so limber at water and timber,
Now on the causeway are fain to be led,
Beat, but still going, a countryman sowing
Has sighted the Lord of the Valley ahead!

There in the bottom, see, sluggish and idle,
Steals the dark stream where the willowtree grows,
Harden your heart and catch hold of your bridle,
Steady him! rouse him! and over he goes.
Look, in a minute a dozen are in it,
But forward! hark forward! for draggled and blown,
A check though desiring, with courage untiring,
The Lord of the Valley is holding his own.

Onward we struggle in sorrow and labour,
Lurching and lobbing, and "bellows to mend",
Each, while he smiles at the plight of his neighbour,
Only is anxious to get to the end.
Horses are flagging, hounds drooping and lagging,
But gathering down yonder, where press as they may,
Mobbed, driven, and haunted, but game and undaunted,
The Lord of the Valley stands proudly at bay.

Now here's to the Baron, and all his supporters,
The thrusters, the skirters, the whole of the tale;
And here's to the fairest of all hunting quarters,
The widest of pastures, three cheers for the Vale!
For the fair lady rider, the rogue who beside her
Finds breath in a gallop his suit to advance,
The hounds for our pleasure, that time us the measure,
The Lord of the Valley that leads us the dance!

G. J. Whyte-Melville

THE ARAB'S FAREWELL TO HIS FAVOURITE STEED

My beautiful! my beautiful! that standest meekly by,
With thy proudly arched and glossy neck, and dark and fiery eye,
Fret not to roam the desert now, with all thy winged speed,
I may not mount on thee again – thou'rt sold, my Arab steed.

Fret not with that impatient hoof – snuff not the breezy wind –
The farther that thou fliest now, so far am I behind;
The stranger hath the bridle-rein – thy master hath his gold –
Fleet-limbed and beautiful, farewell; thou'rt sold, my steed, thou'rt sold.

Farewell! those free, untired limbs full many a mile must roam,
To reach the chill and wintry sky which clouds the stranger's home;
Some other hand, less fond, must now thy corn and bed prepare,
Thy silky mane, I braided once, must be another's care!
The morning sun shall dawn again, but never more with thee
Shall I gallop through the desert paths, where we were wont to be;
Evening shall darken on the earth, and o'er the sandy plain
Some other steed, with slower step, shall bear me home again.

Yes, thou must go! the wild, free breeze, the brilliant sun and sky,
Thy master's house – from all of these my exiled one must fly;
Thy proud dark eye will grow less proud, thy step become less fleet,
And vainly shalt thou arch thy neck thy master's hand to meet.
Only in sleep shall I behold that dark eye, glancing bright; –
Only in sleep shall I hear again that step so firm and light;
And when I raise my dreaming arm to check or cheer thy speed,
Then must I, starting, wake to feel – thou'rt sold my Arab steed!

Ah! rudely then, unseen by me, some cruel hand may chide,
Till foam-wreaths lie, like crested waves, along thy panting side:
And the rich blood that's in thee swells, in thy indignant pain,
Till careless eyes, which rest on thee, may count each starting vein.
Will they ill-use thee? If I thought – but no, it cannot be –
Thou art so swift, yet easy curbed; so gentle, yet so free:
And yet, if haply, when thou'rt gone, my lonely heart should yearn –
Can the hand which cast thee from it now command thee to return?

Return! alas! my Arab steed! what shall thy master do,
When thou, who wast his all of joy, hast vanished from his view?
When the dim distance cheats mine eye, and through the gathering tears,
Thy bright form, for a moment, like a false mirage appears;
Slow and unmounted shall I roam, with weary step alone,
Where with fleet step, and joyous bound, thou oft hast borne me on;
And sitting down by that green well, I'll pause and sadly think,
"It was here he bowed his glossy neck when last I saw him drink!"

When last I saw thee drink! – Away! the fevered dream is o'er –
I could not live a day, and know that we should meet no more!
They tempted me, my beautiful! – for hunger's power is strong –
They tempted me, my beautiful! – but I have loved too long.
Who said that I had given thee up? Who said that thou wast sold?
'Tis false – 'tis false, my Arab steed! I fling them back their gold!
Thus, thus, I leap upon thy back, and scour the distant plains;
Away! who overtakes us now shall claim thee for his pains!

Mrs Norton

RIGHT ROYAL

In a race-course box behind the Stand
Right Royal shone from a strapper's hand.
A big dark bay with a restless tread,
Fetlock deep in a wheat-straw bed;
A noble horse of a nervy blood,
By O Mon Roi out of Rectitude
Something quick in his eye and ear
Gave a hint that he might be queer.
In front, he was all to a horseman's mind;
Some thought him a trifle light behind.
By two good points might his rank be known,
A beautiful head and jumping bone.

He had been the hope of Sir Button Budd,
Who bred him there at the Fletchings stud,
But the Fletchings jockey had flogged him cold.
In a narrow thing as a two-year-old.
After that, with his sulks and swerves,
Dread of the crowd and fits of nerves,
Like a wastrel bee who makes no honey,
He had hardly earned his entry money.

Liking him still, though he failed at racing,
Sir Button trained him for steeple-chasing.
He jumped like a stag, but his heart was cowed;
Nothing would make him face the crowd.
When he reached the Straight where the crowds began
He would make no effort for any man.

Sir Button sold him, Charles Cothill bought him,
Rode him to hounds and soothed and taught him.
After two years' care Charles felt assured
That his horse's broken heart was cured,
And the jangled nerves in tune again.
And now, as proud as a King of Spain,
He moved in his box with a restless tread,
His eyes like sparks in his lovely head,
Ready to run between the roar
Of the stands that face the Straight once more;
Ready to race, though blown, though beat,
As long as his will could lift his feet;
Ready to burst his heart to pass
Each gasping horse in that street of grass.

John Masefield

THE KNIGHT'S LEAP

A Legend of Altenahr

So the foemen have fired the gate, men of mine;
And the water is spent and gone?
Then bring me a cup of red Ahr-wine:
I never shall drink but this one.

And fetch me my harness, and saddle my horse,
And lead him round to the door:
He must take such a leap to-night perforce,
As horse never took before.

I have lived by the saddle for years a score;
And if I must die on a tree,
The old saddle tree, which has borne me of yore,
Is the properest timber for me.

So now to show Bishop, and Burgher, and Priest,
How the Altenahr hawk can die:
If they smoke the old falcon out of his nest,
He must take to his wings and fly.

He harnessed himself by the clear moonshine,
And he mounted his horse at the door;
And he drained such a pull at the red Ahr-wine,
As never man took before.

He spurred the old horse, and he held him tight,
And he leapt him out over the wall;
Out over the cliff, into the night,
Three hundred feet to fall.

They found him next morning below in the glen,
With never a bone in him whole –
Now Mass and a prayer ye good Gentlemen
For such a bold rider's soul.

Charles Kingsley

How We Beat The Favourite

A Lay of the Loamshire Hunt Cup

'Aye, squire,' said Stevens, 'they back him at evens;
The race is all over, bar shouting, they say;
The Clown ought to beat her; Dick Neville is sweeter
Than ever – he swears he can win all the way.

'A gentleman rider – well, I'm an outsider,
But if he's a gent who the mischief's a jock?
You swells mostly blunder, Dick rides for the plunder,
He rides, too, like thunder – he sits like a rock.

'He calls "hunted fairly" a horse that has barely
Been stripp'd for a trot within sight of the hounds,
A horse that at Warwick beat Birdlime and Yorick,
And gave Abdelkader at Aintree nine pounds.

'They say we have no test to warrant a protest;
Dick rides for a lord and stands in with a steward;
The light of their faces they show him – his case is
Prejudged and his verdict already secured.

'But none can outlast her, and few travel faster,
She strides in her work clean way from The Drag,
You hold her and sit her, she couldn't be fitter,
Whenever you hit her she'll spring like a stag.

'And p'rhaps the green jacket, at odds though they back it,
May fall, or there's no knowing what may turn up.
The mare is quite ready, sit still and ride steady,
Keep cool; and I think you may just win the Cup.'

Dark-brown with tan muzzle, just stripped for the tussle,
Stood Iseult, arching her neck to the curb,
A lean head and fiery, strong quarters and wiry,
A loin rather light, but a shoulder superb.

Some parting injunction, bestowed with great unction,
I tried to recall, but forgot like a dunce,
When Reginald Murray, full tilt on White Surrey,
Came down in a hurry to start us at once.

'Keep back in the yellow! Come up on Othello!
Hold hard on the chestnut! Turn round on The Drag!
Keep back there on Spartan! Back you, sir, in tartan!
So, steady there, easy! and down went the flag.

We started, and Kerr made strong running on Mermaid,
Through furrows that led to the first stake-and-bound,
The Track, half extended, look'd bloodlike and splendid,
Held wide on the right where the headland was sound

I pulled hard to baffle her rush with the snaffle,
Before her two-thirds of the field got away;
All through the wet pasture where floods of the last year
Still loitered, they clotted my crimson with clay.

The fourth fence, a wattle, floor'd Monk and Blue-bottle;
The Drag came to grief at the blackthorn and ditch,
The rails toppled over Redoubt and Red Rover,
The lane stopped Lycurgus and Leicestershire Witch.

She passed like an arrow Kildare and Cock Sparrow,
And Mantrap and Mermaid refused the stone wall;
And Giles on The Greyling came down at the paling,
And I was left sailing in front of them all.

I took them a burster, nor eased her nor nursed her
Until the black bullfinch led into the plough,
And through the strong bramble we bored with a scramble –
My cap was knock'd off by the hazel-tree bough.

Where furrows looked lighter I drew the reins tighter –
Her dark chest all dappled with flakes of white foam,
Her flanks mud bespattered, a weak rail she shattered –
We landed on turf with our heads turn'd for home.

Then crash'd a low binder, and then close behind her
The sward to the strokes of the favourite shook;
His rush roused her mettle, yet ever so little
She shorten'd her stride as we raced at the brook.

24

She rose when I hit her, I saw the stream glitter,
A wide scarlet nostril flashed close to my knee,
Between sky and water The Clown came and caught her,
The space that he cleared was a caution to see.

And forcing the running, discarding all cunning,
A length to the front went the rider in green;
A long strip of stubble, and then the big double,
Two stiff flights of rails with a quickset between.

She raced at the rasper, I felt my knees grasp her,
I found my hands give to her strain on the bit,
She rose when The Clown did – our silks as we bounded
Brush'd lightly, our stirrups clash'd loud as we lit.

A rise steeply sloping, a fence with stone coping –
The last – we diverged round the base of the hill;
His path was the nearer, his leap was the clearer,
I flogg'd up the straight, and he led sitting still.

She came to his quarter, and on still I brought her,
And up to his girth, to his breast-plate she drew;
A short prayer from Neville just reach'd me, 'The devil,'
He mutter'd – lock'd level the hurdles we flew.

A hum or hoarse cheering, a dense crowd careering,
All sights seen obscurely, all shouts vaguely heard;
'The green wins!' 'The crimson!' The multitude swims on,
And figures are blended and features are blurr'd.

'The horse is her master!' 'The green forges past her!'
'The Clown will outlast her!' 'The Clown wins!' 'The Clown!'
The white railing races with all the white faces,
The chestnut outpaces, outstretches the brown.

On still past the gateway she strains in the straightway,
Still struggles, 'The Clown by a short neck at most,'
He swerves, the green scourges, the stand rocks and surges,
And flashes, and verges, and flits the white post.

Aye! so ends the tussle – I knew the tan muzzle
Was first, though the ring-men were yelling 'Dead heat'
A nose I could swear by, but Clarke said 'The mare by
A short head.' And that's how the favourite was beat.

Adam Lindsay Gordon

A Rum One To Follow, A Bad One To Beat

Come, I'll give you the health of a man we all know,
A man we all swear by, a friend of our own,
With the hounds running hardest, he's safest to go,
And he's always in front, and he's often alone.
A rider unequalled – a sportsman complete,
A rum one to follow, a bad one to beat.

As he sits in the saddle, a baby could tell
He can hustle a sticker, a flyer can spare,
He has science, and nerve, and decision as well,
He knows where he's going and means to be there.
The first day I saw him they said at the meet,
"That's a rum one to follow, a bad one to beat."

We threw off at the Castle, we found in the holt,
Like wildfire the beauties went streaming away,
From the rest of the field he came out like a bolt,
And he tackled to work like a schoolboy to play,
As he rammed down his hat, and got home in his seat,
This rum one to follow, this bad one to beat.

'Twas a caution, I vow, but to see the man ride!
O'er the rough and the smooth he went sailing along;
And what Providence sent him, he took in his stride,
Though the ditches were deep, and the fences were strong.
Thinks I, "If he leads me I'm in for a treat,
With this rum one to follow, this bad one to beat!"

Ere they'd run for a mile, there was room in the front,
Such a scatter and squander you never did see!
And I honestly own I'd been out of the hunt,
But the broad of his back was the beacon for me.
So I kept him in sight, and was proud of the feat,
This rum one to follow, this bad one to beat!

Till we came to a rasper as black as your hat,
You couldn't see over – you couldn't see through,
So he made for the gate, knowing what he was at,
And the chain being round it, why – over he flew!
While I swore a round oath that I needn't repeat,
At this rum one to follow, this bad one to beat.

For a place I liked better I hastened to seek,
But the place I like better I sought for in vain;
And I honestly own, if the truth I must speak,
That I never caught sight of my leader again.
But I thought, "I'd give something to have his receipt,"
This rum one to follow, this bad one to beat.

They told me that night he went best through the run,
They said that he hung up a dozen to dry,
When a brook in the bottom stopped most of their fun,
But I know that I never went near it, not I.
For I found it a fruitless attempt to compete
With this rum one to follow, this bad one to beat.

So we'll fill him a bumper as deep as you please,
And we'll give him a cheer, for deny it who can,
When the country is roughest he's most at his ease,
When the run is severest, he rides like a man.
And the pace cannot stop, nor the fences defeat,
This rum one to follow, this bad one to beat. .

G. J. Whyte-Melville

29

BY FLOOD AND FIELD

A Legend of the Cotswold

I remember the lowering wintry morn,
And the mist on the Cotswold hills,
Where I once heard the blast of the huntsman's horn,
Not far from the seven rills.

Jack Esdale was there, and Hugh St. Clair,
Bob Chapman and Andrew Kerr,
And big George Griffiths on Devil-May Care,
And – black Tom Oliver.
And one who rode on a dark-brown steed,
Clean jointed, sinewy, spare,
With the lean game head of the Blacklock breed,
And the resolute eye that loves the lead,
And the quarters massive and square –
A tower of strength, with a promise of speed
(There was Celtic blood in the pair).

I remember how merry a start we got,
When the red fox broke from the gorse,
In a country so deep, with a scent so hot,
That the hound could outpace the horse;
I remember how few in the front rank show'd
How endless appeared the tail,
On the brown hill side, where we cross'd the road,
And headed towards the vale.
The dark-brown steed on the left was there,
On the right was a dappled grey,
And between the pair, on a chestnut mare,
The duffer who writes this lay.

What business had 'this child' there to ride?
But little or none at all;
Yet I held my own for a while in 'the pride
That goeth before a fall'.
Though rashness can hope for but one result,
We are heedless when fate draws nigh us,
And the maxim holds good, 'Quem perdere vult
Deus, dementat prius.'

The right hand man to the left hand said,
As down in the vale we went,
'Harden your heart like a millstone, Ned,
And set your face as flint;
Solid and tall is the rasping wall
That stretches before us yonder;
You must have it at speed or not at all,
'Twere better to halt than to ponder,
For the stream runs wide on the take-off side,
And washes the clay bank under;
Here goes for a pull, 'tis a madman's ride,
And a broken neck if you blunder.'

No word in reply his comrade spoke,
Nor waver'd nor once look'd round,
But I saw him shorten his horse's stroke
As we splash'd through the marshy ground;
I remember the laugh that all the while
On his quiet features play'd: –
So he rode to his death, with that careless smile,
In the van of the 'Light Brigade';

So stricken by Russian grape, the cheer
Rang out, while he toppled back,
From the shattered lungs as merry and clear
As it did when it roused the pack.
Let never a tear his memory stain,
Give his ashes never a sigh,
One of many who perished, NOT IN VAIN,
AS A TYPE OF OUR CHIVALRY –

I remember one thrust he gave to his hat,
And two to the flanks of the brown,
And still as a statue of old he sat,
And he shot to the front, hands down;
I remember the snort and the stag-like bound
Of the steed six lengths to the fore,
And the laugh of the rider while, landing sound,
He turned in his saddle and glanced around;
I remember – but little more,
Save a bird's-eye gleam of the dashing stream
A jarring thud on the wall,
A shock and the blank of a nightmare's dream –
I was down with a stunning fall.

Adam Lindsay Gordon

BOLTS

I've a head like a violin-case; I've a jaw like a piece of steel;
I've a mouth like india-rubber, and devil a bit I feel;
So I've had my fun with a biped thing that clambered upon my back,
And I'm in at the death, though I'm panting for breath, right bang in the
   midst of the pack.

With a cockney sportsman mounted on top,
That has hired me out for the day,
It's the moment for me to be off for a spree
In a new and original way.
In my own most original way.
Oats! but my spirits were gay!
When I betted my bit that my rider should sit
Somewhere else ere the close of the day.

I started a gentle canter; I felt him bob about,
His spurs went in, and the roots of sin, they whipped my hind legs out.
He put his arms around my neck, 'twas kindly meant, I swear,
But he had no call to spoil it all by pulling out half my hair.

He left his hat in a puddle, he left his whip on a gate,
The briars knew where, but I don't care, the bits of his tunic wait;
He bade me stay, I raced away, to the sound of the huntsman's horn,
And at last I laid him gently in the arms of a bold blackthorn.

The whip waits safe in the harness-room, the groom in the stable yard,
It's not that I mind a tanning – my hide's grown far too hard –
But that tied to a fly I'm safe to die, and on chaff and straw abstain,
For sure as I snort, if they give me this sort, of course I shall do it again.

With a cockney sportsman mounted on top,
That has hired me out for the day
It's the moment for me to be off for a spree
In a new and original way.
In my own most original way.
Oats! but my spirits were gay!
When I betted my bit that my rider should sit,
Somewhere else ere the close of the day.

Anonymous

THE GOOD GREY MARE

Dedicated to the Honourable Robert Grimston, in kindly remembrance of
many happy days and pleasant rides

Oh! once I believed in a woman's kiss,
I had faith in a flattering tongue,
For lip to lip was a promise of bliss,
When lips were smooth and young.
But now the beard is grey on my cheek,
And the top of my head gets bare,
So little I speak, like an Arab sheikh,
But put my trust in my mare.

For loving looks grow hard and cold,
Fair heads are turned away,
When the fruit has been gathered – the talk been told,
And the dog has had his day;
But chance and change 'tis folly to rue,
And say I, the devil may care!
Nor grey nor blue are so bonny and true,
As the bright brown eye of my mare!

It is good for a heart that is chilled and sad
With the death of a vain desire,
To borrow a glow that shall make it glad
From the warmth of a kindred fire.
And I leap to the saddle, a man indeed
For all I can do and dare,
In the power and speed that are mine at need,
While I sit on the back of my mare!

With the fair wide heaven above outspread
The fair wide plain to meet,
With the lark and his carol high over my head,
And the bustling pack at my feet, –
I feel no fetter, I know no bounds,
I am free as a bird in the air;
While the covert resounds, in a chorus of hounds,
Right under the nose of the mare.

We are in for a gallop – away! away!
I told them my beauty could fly;
And we'll lead them a dance ere they catch us today,
For we mean it, my lass and I!
She skims the fences, she scours the plain,
Like a creature winged, I swear,
With snort and strain, on the yielding rein;
For I'm bound to humour the mare.

They have pleached it strong, they have dug it wide,
They have turned the baulk with the plough;
A horse that can cover the whole in its stride
Is cheap at a thousand, I vow;
So I draw her together, and over we sail,
With a yard and a half to spare –
Bank, bullfinch, and rail – 'tis the Curse of the vale,
But I leave it all to the mare!

Away! away! they've been running to kill,
With never a check from the find;
Away, away! we are close to them still,
And the field are furlongs behind!
They can hardly deny they were out of the game,
Lost half "the fun of the fair",
Though the envious blame and the jealous exclaim,
"How that old fool buckets his mare!"

Who-whoop! they have him – they're round him; how
They worry and tear when he's down!
'Twas a stout hill-fox when they found him, now
'Tis a hundred tatters of brown!
And the riders arriving as best they can,
In panting plight, declare,
That "First in the van was the old grey man,
Who stands by his old grey mare".

I have lived my life – I am nearly done –
I have played the game all round;
But I freely admit that the best of my fun
I owe it to horse and hound.
With a hopeful heart and a conscience clear,
I can laugh in your face, Black Care;
Though you're hovering near, there's not room for you here,
On the back of my good grey mare.

G. J. Whyte-Melville

THE OLD BROWN HORSE

The old brown horse looks over the fence
In a weary sort of way;
He seems to be saying to all who pass:
"Well, folks, I've had my day –
I'm simply watching the world go by,
And nobody seems to mind,
As they're dashing past in their motor-cars,
A horse who is lame and half-blind."

The old brown horse has a shaggy coat,
But once he was young and trim,
And he used to trot through the woods and lanes
With the man who was fond of him.
But his master rides in a motor-car,
And it makes him feel quite sad
When he thinks of the days that used to be,
And of all the times they had.

Sometimes a friendly soul will stop
Near the fence, where the tired old head
Rests wearily on the topmost bar,
And a friendly word is said.
Then the old brown horse gives a little sigh
As he feels the kindly touch
Of a hand on his mane or his shaggy coat,
And he doesn't mind so much.

So if you pass by the field one day,
Just stop for a word or two.
With the old brown horse who was once as young
And as full of life as you.
He'll love the touch of your soft young hand,
And I know he'll seem to say –
"Oh, thank you, friend, for the kindly thought
For a horse who has had his day."

W. F. Holmes

A BUTTY LITTLE ONE

I've a butty little one in my stable,
I've a butty little one that can fly,
And my butty little one is well able
To be there when a beat fox dies.
I've a butty little one that can jump, Sir,
I've a butty little one that can stay,
If you want to be up in the front, Sir,
Just ride my butty little grey.
Though I've many good steeds in my stable
Of Chestnut, Black and Bay,
I'll drink with most vigour at the table
To my brave little, butty little grey.

Patrick Hore-Ruthven

THE PLACE WHERE
THE OLD HORSE DIED

In the hollow, by the pollard, where the crop is tall and rank
Of the dock-leaf and the nettle growing free,
Where the bramble and the brushwood straggle blindly o'er the
    bank,
And the pyat jerks and chatters on the tree,
There's a fence I never pass
In the sedges and the grass,
But for very shame I turn my head aside,
While the tears come thick and hot,
And my curse is on the spot –
'Tis the place where the old horse died.

There's his hoof upon the chimney, there's his hide upon the chair,
A better never bent him to the rein;
Now, for all my love and care, I've an empty stall and bare;
I shall never ride my gallant horse again!
How he laid him out at speed,
How he loved to have a lead,
How he snorted in his mettle and his pride!
Not a flyer of the Hunt
Was beside him in the front,
At the place where the old horse died!

Was he blown? I hardly think it. Did he slip?
I cannot tell.
We had run for forty minutes in the vale,
He was reaching at his bridle; he was going strong and well,
And he never seemed to falter or to fail;
Though I some times fancy, too,
That his daring spirit knew

The task beyond the compass of his stride,
Yet he faced it true and brave,
And dropped into his grave
At the place where the old horse died!

I was up in half a minute, but he never seemed to stir,
Though I scored him with my rowels in the fall;
In his life he had not felt before the insult of the spur;
And I knew that it was over once for all.
When motionless he lay
In his cheerless bed of clay,
Huddled up without an effort on his side –
'Twas a hard and bitter stroke,
For his honest back was broke,
At the place where the old horse died.

With a neigh so faint and feeble that it touched me like a groan,
"Farewell," he seemed to murmur, "ere I die";
Then set his teeth and stretched his limbs, and so I stood alone,
While the merry chase went heedless sweeping by.
Am I womanly and weak
If the tear was on my cheek
For a brotherhood that death could thus divide?
If sickened and amazed
Through a woeful mist I gazed
On the place where the old horse died?

There are men both good and wise who hold that in a future state
Dumb creatures we have cherished here below
Shall give us joyous greeting when we pass the golden gate;
Is it folly that I hope it may be so?
For never man had friend
More enduring to the end,
Truer mate in every turn of time and tide.
Could I think we'd meet again
It would lighten half my pain
At the place where the old horse died.

G. J. Whyte-Melville

K. E. Newcome-Baker

Two gentlemen met, both unhors'd, in a lane
(Foxhunting on foot is but labour in vain)
"Have you seen a brown horse?" "No, indeed, Sir; but pray,
In the course of your ramble have you seen a Grey?"

R. R. Egerton Warburton

LORRAINE, LORRAINE, LORÈE

'Are you read for your steeple-chase, Lorraine, Lorraine, Lorrèe?
You're booked to ride your capping race today at Coulterlee,
You're booked to ride *Vindictive*, for all the world to see,
To keep him straight, to keep him first, and win the run for me."

She clasped her new-born baby, poor Lorraine, Lorraine, Lorrèe,
"I cannot ride *Vindictive*, as any man might see,
And I will not ride *Vindictive* with this baby on my knee.
He's killed a boy, he's killed a man, and why must he kill me?'

"Unless you ride *Vindictive*, Lorraine, Lorraine, Lorrèe,
Unless you ride *Vindictive* today at Coulterlee,
And land him safe across the brook, and win the race for me,
It's you may keep your baby, for you'll get no keep from me."

"That husbands could be cruel," said Lorraine, Lorraine, Lorrèe,
"That husbands could be cruel, I have known for seasons three;
But oh! to ride *Vindictive* while a baby cries for me,
And be killed across a fence at last for all the world to see!"

She mastered young *Vindictive* – Oh! the gallant lass was she,
And kept him straight and won the race as near as near could be;
But he killed her at the brook against a pollard willow-tree,
Oh! he killed her at the brook, the brute, for all the world to see,
And no one but the baby cried for poor Lorraine, Lorrèe.

Charles Kingsley

Probably the last poem he wrote, in 1874 in Colorado

THE CAPTAINS

One was a Lancer, long of limb,
And it took a good 'un to ride with him;
The other a Guardsman, extra bold,
He liked a horse that would take a hold;
He liked a country strongly fenced
And a solid pace when the play commenced;
With a travelling fox and a serving scent
There were few could follow the way he went.

Many a run did these heroes see,
Riding it jealously knee to knee;
Many a fence did they cross together
With a touch of steel and a scrape of leather;
Many a time did the Lancer land
With the Guardsman's whip in his bridle hand;
Many a time was the air turned blue
By the curses flying between the two.

The fields had been gripped in a four weeks' frost,
The best of the season was over and lost,
When the country woke to a welcome thaw
And horses could gallop and hounds could draw,
And spoiling for work the Captains came
With an added zest for their favourite game,
Cantering up through the spattering mud,
Chaffing each other and out for blood.

Scarcely had hounds o'er the fence-top flung
When a wise old bitch in the whins gave tongue;
The huntsman cheered her; another spoke;
The sterns in a green world waved like smoke.

The Lancer swung through the bridle gate,
The Guardsman roared to him: 'D—n you, wait!'
Then, as he heard the 'Gone away!'
Rammed the spurs in his plunging bay.

The Master shouted a vain reproof,
A clod of dirt from the blood one's hoof
Plastered his mouth, and before he had cursed
They were both of them off, with the Lancer first.
As huntsman and hounds poured out of the whin
Stirrup to stirrup the two cut in;
And over the vale strung out the chase
With the Captains sharing the foremost place.

Both were over the first fence well,
The Guardsman muttering, 'What the hell
Is the use of gettin' in front of hounds?'
And the Lancer shouting, 'A thousand pounds
Wouldn't buy this steeplechase horse of mine,
And, d—n your eyes, will you keep your line!'
And the Guardsman crammed on extra speed
And bumped his rival and took the lead.

The Lancer swayed, but he kept on deck,
And they raced up the pasture neck to neck;
The grey horse snatched and the bay took hold,
And they lashed at a bullfinch, jumping bold;
The Guardsman broke through the boughs a track,
And the Lancer swore as the twigs swung back,
And the bay drew out and forged ahead
And over the furrows the Guardsman led.

The bay horse steadied and cocked an ear
As a hedge and a yawning ditch drew near;
As he rose at the jump the bank gave way
And into the water he slipped and lay.
His rider, wet to the waistcoat, stood
And cursed as a cut-away Captain should,
While over his head the Lancer flew,
Shouting, 'An excellent place for you!'

And that was the end of Lance *v.* Sword,
For each attained to his just reward
By duly wedding a charming wife
Who would not allow him to risk his life;
And now you may watch those two to-day
Meet at a gate, with a fox away,
And see them bowing each other through,
And hear them murmuring, 'After you!'

W. H. Ogilvie

NICHOLAS NYE

Thistle and darnel and dock grew there,
And a bush, in the corner, of may,
On the orchard wall I used to sprawl
In the blazing heat of the day;
Half asleep and half awake,
While the birds went twittering by,
And nobody there my lone to share
But Nicholas Nye.

Nicholas Nye was lean and grey,
Lame of a leg and old,
More than a score of donkey's years
He had seen since he was foaled;
He munched the thistles, purple and spiked,
Would sometimes stoop and sigh,
And turn to his head, as if he said,
"Poor Nicholas Nye!"

Alone with his shadow he'd drowse in the meadow,
Lazily swinging his tail,
At break of day he used to bray –
Not much too hearty and hale;
But a wonderful gumption was under his skin,
And a clean calm light in his eye,
And once in a while, he'd smile –
Would Nicholas Nye.

Seem to be smiling at me, he would,
From his bush, in the corner, of may –
Bony and ownerless, widowed and worn,
Knobble-kneed, lonely and grey;
And over the grass would seem to pass
'Neath the deep dark blue of the sky,
Something much better than words between, me
And Nicholas Nye

But dark would come in the apple boughs,
The green of the glow-worm shine,
The birds in nest would crouch to rest,
And home I'd trudge to mine;
And there, in the moonlight, dark with dew,
Asking not wherefore nor why,
Would brood like a ghost, and as still as a post,
Old Nicholas Nye.

Walter de la Mare

THE DONKEY

When fishes flew and forests walked
And figs grew upon thorn,
Some moment when the moon was blood
Then surely I was born;

With monstrous head and sickening cry
And ears like errant wings,
The devil's walking parody
On all four-footed things.

The tattered outlaw of the earth,
Of ancient crooked will;
Starve, scourge, deride me: I am dumb,
I keep my secret still.

Fools! For I also had my hour;
One far fierce hour and sweet:
There was a shout about my ears,
And palms before my feet.

                              G. K. Chesterton

HARD-RIDING DICK

From the cradle his name has been "Hard-riding Dick",
Since the time when cock-horse he bestraddled a stick;
Since the time, when unbreached, without saddle or rein;
He'd kick'd the old Jackass along the green lane.

Dick, wasting no time o'er the classical page,
Spent his youth in the stable without any wage;
The life of poor Dick, when he enter'd his teens,
Was to sleep in the hay-loft and breakfast on beans.

Promoted at length, Dick's adventures began –
A stripling on foot, but when mounted a man;
Capp'd, booted and spurr'd, his young soul was on fire;
The day he was dubb'd "Second Whip" to the Squire.

See, how Dick, like a dart, shoots ahead of the pack!
How he stops, turns, and twists, rates and rattles them back!
The laggard exciting, controlling the rash,
He can comb down a hair with the point of his lash.

Oh, show me that country which Dick cannot cross –
Be it open or wood, be it upland or moss,
Through the fog or the sunshine, the calm or the squall,
By daylight or starlight, or no light at all!

Like a swallow can Dick o'er the water-flood skim,
And Dick like a duck, in the saddle can swim;
Up the steep mountain side like a cat he can crawl,
He can squeeze like a mouse through a hole in the wall!

He can tame a wild young one, inspirit the old,
The restive, the runaway, handle and hold;
Sharp steel or soft-sawder, whiche'er does the trick,
It makes little matter to Hard-riding Dick.

Bid the chief from the Desert bring hither his mare,
To ride o'er the plain against Dick if he dare;
Bring Cossack or Mexican, Spaniard or Gaul,
There's a Dick in our village will ride round them all!

A whip is Dick's sceptre, a saddle Dick's throne,
A horse is the kingdom he rules as own;
While grasping ambition encircles the earth,
The dominions of Dick are enclosed in a girth.

Three ribs hath he broken, two legs and one arm,
But there hangs, it is said, round his neck a life-charm;
Still long odds are offer'd that Dick, when he drops,
Will die as he lived, in his breaches and tops.

R. R. Egerton Warburton

THE BALLAD OF THE FOXHUNTER

Lay me in a cushioned chair;
Carry me, ye four,
With cushions here and cushions there,
To see the world once more.

'To stable and to kennel go;
Bring what is there to bring;
Lead my Lollard to and fro,
Or gently in a ring.

'Put the chair upon the grass:
Bring Rody and his hounds,
That I may contented pass
From these earthly bounds.'

His eyelids droop, his head falls low,
His old eyes cloud with dreams;
The sun upon all things that grow
Falls in sleepy streams.

Brown Lollard treads upon the lawn,
And to the armchair goes,
And now the old man's dreams are gone,
He smooths the long brown nose.

And now moves many a pleasant tongue
Upon his wasted hands,
For leading aged hounds and young
The huntsman near him stands.

'Huntsman Rody, blow the horn,
Make the hills reply.'
The huntsman loosens on the morn
A gay wandering cry.

Fire is in the old man's eyes,
His fingers move and sway,
And when the wandering music dies
They hear him feebly say,

'Huntsman Rody, blow the horn,
Make the hills reply.'
'I cannot blow upon my horn,
I can but weep and sigh.'

Servants round his cushioned place
Are with new sorrow wrung;
Hounds are gazing on his face,
Aged hounds and young.

One blind hound only lies apart
On the sun-smitten grass;
He holds deep commune with his heart:
The moments pass and pass;

The blind hound with a mournful din
Lifts slow his wintry head;
The servants bear the body in;
The hounds wail for the dead.

W. B. Yeates

THE LITTLE HORSE

He's not very big – stands a bare 15·2 –
But he's wiry and tough and he knows what to do.
He's hunted the fox and he's hunted the stag –
Done a bit of show-jumping and gone with the Drag;
He's not very fast and he's not very slow,
But he's quick, and he's bold, and he never says "No!"
And – knowing his job from the A to the Z,
And having a cartful of brains in his head,
And also a genuine love of the game –
You can truthfully say that there's no one to blame
But yourself, if he's not at the top of the hunt –
And – if you know your job – you can both be in front.

A. F. D.

THE AMATEUR RIDER

Him going to ride for us! *Him* – with the pants and the eyeglass and all.
Amateur! don't he just look it – it's twenty to one on a fall.
Boss must be gone off his head to be sending our steeplechase crack
Out over fences like these with an object like that on his back.

Ride! Don't tell *me* he can ride. With his pants just as loose as balloons,
How can he sit on his horse? and his spurs like a pair of harpoons;
Ought to be under the Dog Act, he ought, and be kept off the course.
Fall! Why, he'd fall off a cart, let alone off a steeplechase horse.
Yessir! the 'orse is all ready – I wish you'd have rode him before;
Nothing like knowing your 'orse, sir, and this chap's a terror to bore;
Battleaxe always could pull, and he rushes his fences like fun –
Stands off his jump twenty feet, and then springs like a shot from a gun.

Oh, he can jump 'em all right, sir, you make no mistake, 'e's a toff;
Clouts 'em in earnest, too, sometimes, you mind that he don't clout you
    off –
Don't seem to mind how he hits 'em, his shins is as hard as a nail,
Sometimes you'll see the fence shake and the splinters fly up from the rail.

All you can do is to hold him and just let him jump as he likes,
Give him his head at the fences, and hang on like death if he strikes;
Don't let him run himself out – you can lie third or fourth in the race –
Until you clear the stone wall, and from that you can put on the pace.

Fell at that wall once, he did, and it gave him a regular spread,
Ever since that time he flies it – he'll stop if you pull at his head,
Just let him race – you can trust him – he'll take first-class care he don't
    fall,
And I think that's the lot – but remember, *he must have his head at the wall.*

60

Well, he's down safe as far as the start, and he seems to sit on pretty neat,
Only his baggified breeches would ruinate anyone's seat –
They're away – here they come – the first fence, and he's head over heels
   for a crown!
Good for the new chum, he's over, and two of the others are down!

Now for the treble, my hearty – By Jove, he can ride, after all;
Whoop, that's your sort – let him fly them! He hasn't much fear of a fall.
Who in the world would have thought it? And aren't they just going a
   pace?
Little Recruit in the lead there will make it a stoutly-run race.

Lord! But they're racing in earnest – and down goes Recruit on his head,
Rolling clean over his boy – it's a miracle if he ain't dead.
Battleaxe, Battleaxe yet! By the Lord, he's got most of 'em beat –
Ho! did you see how he struck, and the swell never moved in his seat?

Second time round, and, by Jingo! he's holding his lead of 'em well;
Hark to him clouting the timber! It don't seem to trouble the swell.
Now for the wall – let him rush it. A thirty-foot leap, I declare –
Never a shift in his seat, and he's racing for home like a hare.

What's that that's chasing him – Rataplan – regular demon to stay!
Sit down and ride for your life now! Oh, good, that's the style – come
  away!
Rataplan's certain to beat you, unless you can give him the slip;
Sit down and rub in the whalebone – now give him the spurs and the
  whip!

Battleaxe, Battleaxe, yet – and it's Battleaxe wins for a crown;
Look at him rushing the fences, he wants to bring t'other chap down.
Rataplan never will catch him if only he keeps on his pins;
Now! the last fence! and he's over it! Battleaxe, Battleaxe wins!

Well, sir, you rode him just perfect – I knew from the first you could ride.
Some of the chaps said you couldn't, an' I says just like this a' one side:
Mark me, I says, that's a tradesman – the saddle is where he was bred.
Weight! you're all right, sir, and thank you; and them was the words that I
  said.

'Banjo' Paterson

63

STEEPLECHASERS

Tucked away in winter quarters,
Gainsborough's sons and Buchan's daughters,
Blue of blood, clean-lined and handsome,
Priced beyond a prince's ransom,
Where no danger can befall them
Rest till next year's Classics call them;
And the limber lean-of-head ones,
Hardy, hefty, humble-bred ones,
Booted, bandaged to the knee,
Ready for whate'er may be,
Gallant slaves and cheery martyrs,
Stand once more before the starters.

Piggotts, Masons, Leaders, Dullers
Witch the word in mud-splashed colours,
Brushing through the birchwood switches,
Cramming at the open ditches,
Grinning when the guard-rails rattle
In the fore-front of the battle.
Gordons, Anthonys and Reeses
Bow their heads against the breezes,
Hail upon their faces whipping,
Wet reins through their fingers slipping
As they drive their 'chasers crashing
Through the fence-tops, irons clashing.

So they forge through wind and weather
To the crack of straining leather
Lashing at the leaps together,
With the fluttering flags to guide them,
Taking what the Fates provide them,
Danger calling, Death beside them –
'Tis a game beyond gainsaying
Made by gods for brave men's playing.

W. H. Ogilvie

THE SPARE RIDE

When they asked me to ride one at Riddlemaree,
I said, "I'm no jockey, so why come to me?"
And then they explained (and it filled me with pride)
That this was a horse that no jockey could ride.

Now I know very well, as I'd always been taught,
That jockeys ride badly with stirrups too short.
It's my natural seat and my delicate hands.
As I've often discovered, a horse understands.
And this is a fact you must all of you know
Who have watched me in London perform in the Row.

When we got to the course it was rainy and cold,
And (though sure of success) I felt rather less bold.
And some fiend of a friend of the owner's I met
Said, "I'm sorry, young feller, your reins will be wet,
When your reins are all wet and your hands are all cold,
It's a horrible game when they do take a hold;
But never you worry, young feller me lad,
You *can't* have worse purlers than some that I've had."

The trainer's instructions were rapid and brief –
"Not a lot to remember," I thought with relief.
"Now lie about third, and you know what to do –
If you don't pull at him he won't pull at you."
I answered, "That's right; I'm a horseman, you see,
And I shan't pull at him and he won't pull at me."
And I thought of the words of my father – how true –
"If you don't pull at them they won't pull at you."
Though a thought to my mind came unpleasantly grim –
He *may* pull at me though I don't pull at him!
And I wished that I'd asked, in the past, clever men,
"If he *does* pull at me what ought I do then?"

Then a horrible boy as he tightened the girth
Said, "'Ang on to 'im, guv'ner, for all that yer worth,
For I rides 'im at 'ome, and I'll tell yer 'e's fit,
And I'm telling yer, guv'ner, *'e 'angs on a bit.*"

We cantered to post at a horrible pace –
A speed that seemed suited to winning a race.
And I thought to myself, "What a silly idea
Not to start from the paddock. Why send us out here?"
And the wind and the rain made me splutter and cough;
I'd half lengthened one leather, and then we were off.
The trainer's instructions were clearly absurd –
If two others won't pass you how can you lie third?

We came to the first, and I threw all my weight
On the reins, which alone could save me from my fate.
And the next we went over, the next we went through,
And the next was the ditch: something told me – I knew.
But I wrestled no longer, my hands were too chilled,
And I thought, "Does it hurt very much to be killed?"

But the time had gone by to consider these things;
He took off with a bound as we came in the wings.
And between the first crash and the ultimate blow
I saw for a moment the sky – down below.

One would think, when a body lies prone on the ground.
That compassion would make other jockeys pull round.
But no! As I struggled attempting to rise
They approached and one shouted, "Keep still, blast your eyes!"

But soon with a crash and a thunder they passed,
I rose to my feet – it was over at last.
But I did not walk back; for a spell I remained
Extremely upset from the shock I'd sustained.
And I thought, "I'll let men come and render first aid
That's what they are there for and why they are paid."
Though I waited a little no ambulance came
And I found that the owner for this was to blame.
For he'd seen the whole thing through his glasses and said,
"There's no need to fetch him – the blighter's not dead."

But I thought then of others; unless I returned
The crowd might be anxious and getting concerned.
It was clearly a duty for which I must strive
To return and to tell them that I was alive.
But that friend of the owner's, a man that I hate,
As I entered the paddock was just by the gate.
And as I limped past him all plastered with dirt
He said, "By the way, was the horse at all hurt?"

While the owner was not sympathetic at all;
He didn't allude to my horrible fall.
But said, "Why were you rolling about? Were you cracked?
Supposing you'd brought down the one that we'd backed!"

M. U. G.

The poem appeared in *Horse and Hound* fifty years ago.

FATHER RILEY'S HORSE

'Twas the horse thief, Andy Regan, that was hunted like a dog
By the troopers of the Upper Murray side,
They had searched in every gully – they had looked in every bog,
But never sight or track of him they spied,
Till the priest at Kiley's Crossing heard a knocking very late
And a whisper 'Father Riley – come across!'
So his Rev'rence in pyjamas trotted softly to the gate
And admitted Andy Regan – and a horse!

'Now, it's listen, Father Riley, to the words I've got to say,
'For its close upon my death I am to-night.
'With the troopers hard behind me I've been hiding all the day
'In the gullies keeping close and out of sight.
'But they're watching all the ranges till there's not a bird could fly,
'And I'm fairly worn to pieces with the strife,
'So I'm taking no more trouble, but I'm going home to die,
'Tis the only way I see to save my life.

'Yes, I'm making home to mother's, and I'll die o' Tuesday next
'An' be buried on the Thursday – and, of course,
'I'm prepared to meet my penance, but with one thing I'm perplexed
'And it's – Father, it's this jewel of a horse!
'He was never bought nor paid for, and there's not a man can swear
'To his owner or his breeder, but I know
'That his sire was by Pedantic from the Old Pretender mare
'And his dam was close related to The Roe.

'And there's nothing in the district that can race him for a step,
'He could canter while they're going at the top:
'He's the king of all the leppers that was ever seen to lep,
'A five-foot fence – he'd clear it in a hop!
'So I'll leave him with you, Father, till the dead shall rise again,
'Tis yourself that knows a good 'un; and, of course,
'You can say he's got by Moonlight out of Paddy Murphy's plain
'If you're ever asked the breeding of the horse!

'But it's getting on to daylight and it's time to say good-bye,
'For the stars above the East are growing pale.
'And I'm making home to mother – and it's hard for me to die!
'But it's harder still, is keeping out of gaol!
'You can ride the old horse over to my grave across the dip
'Where the wattle bloom is waving overhead.
'Sure he'll jump them fences easy – you must never raise the whip
'Or he'll rush 'em! – now, goodbye!' and he had fled!

So they buried Andy Regan, and they buried him to rights,
In the graveyard at the back of Kiley's Hill;
There were five-and-twenty mourners who had five-and-twenty fights
Till the very boldest fighters had their fill.
There were fifty horses racing from the graveyard to the pub,
And their riders flogged each other all the while.
And the lashins of the liquor! And the lavins of the grub!
Oh, poor Andy went to rest in proper style.

Then the races came to Kiley's – with a steeplechase and all,
For the folk were mostly Irish round about,
And it takes an Irish rider to be fearless of a fall,
They were training morning in and morning out.
But they never started training till the sun was on the course
For a superstitious story kept 'em back,
That the ghost of Andy Regan on a slashing chestnut horse,
Had been training by the starlight on the track.

And they read the nomination for the races with surprise
And amusement at the Father's little joke,
For a novice had been entered for the steeplechasing prize,
And they found that it was Father Riley's moke!
He was neat enough to gallop, he was strong enough to stay!
But his owner's views of training were immense,
For the Reverend Father Riley used to ride him every day,
And he never saw a hurdle nor a fence.

And the priest would join the laughter; 'Oh,' said he, 'I put him in,
'For there's five and twenty sovereigns to be won.
'And the poor would find it useful, if the chestnut chanced to win,
'And he'll maybe win when all is said and done!'
He had called him Faugh-a-ballagh, which is French for clear the course,
And his colours were a vivid shade of green:
All the Dooleys and O'Donnells were on Father Riley's horse,
While the Orangemen were backing Mandarin!

It was Hogan, the dog poisoner – aged man and very wise,
Who was camping in the racecourse with his swag
And who ventured an opinion, to the township's great surprise,
That the race would go to Father Riley's nag.
'You can talk about your riders – and the horse has not been schooled,
'And the fences is terrific, and the rest!
'When the field is fairly going, then ye'll see ye've all been fooled,
'And the chestnut horse will battle with the best.

'For there's some has got condition, and they think the race is sure,
'And the chestnut horse will fall beneath the weight,
'But the hopes of all the helpless, and the prayers of all the poor,
'Will be running by his side to keep him straight.
'And it's what's the need of schoolin' or of workin' on the track,
'When the saints are there to guide him round the course!
'I've prayed him over every fence – I've prayed him out and back!
'And I'll bet my cash on Father Riley's horse!'

Oh, the steeple was a caution! They went tearin' round and round,
And the fences rang and rattled where they struck.
There was some that cleared the water – there was more fell in and
  drowned,
Some blamed the men and others blamed the luck!
But the whips were flying freely when the field came into view,
For the finish down the long green stretch of course,
And in front of all the flyers – jumpin' like a kangaroo,
Came the rank outsider – Father Riley's horse!
And old Hogan muttered sagely, 'If it wasn't for the beard
'They'd be thinking it was Andy Reagan's self!'

And the poor of Kiley's Crossing drank the health at Christmastide
Of the chestnut and his rider dressed in green.
There was never such a rider, not since Andy Regan died,
And they wondered who on earth he could have been.
But they settled it among 'em, for the story got about,
'Mongst the bushmen and the people on the course,
That the Devil had been ordered to let Andy Regan out
For the steeplechase on Father Riley's horse!

'Banjo' Paterson

73

THE FOX MEDITATES

When Samson set my brush a' fire,
To spoil the Timnites' barley,
I made my point for Leicestershire,
And left Philistia early.
Through Gath and Rankesborough Gorse, I fled,
And took the Coplow Road, sir!
And was a Gentleman in Red
when all the Quorn wore woad, sir!

When Rome lay massed on Hadrian's Wall,
And nothing much was doing,
Her bored Centurions heard my call
O' nights when I went wooing.
They raised a pack – they ran it well
(For I was there to run 'em)
From Aesica to Carter Fell,
And down North Tyne to Hunnum.

When William landed, hot for blood,
And Harold's hosts were smitten,
I lay at earth in Battle Wood
While Domesday Book was written.
Whatever harm he did to man,
I owe him pure affection,
For in his righteous reign began
The first of Game protection.

When Charles, my namesake, lost his mask,
And Oliver dropped his'n,
I set those Northern Squires a task,
To keep 'em out of prison.
In boots as big as milking-pails,
With holsters on the pommel,
They chevied me across the Dales
Instead of fighting Cromwell.

When thrifty Walpole took the helm,
And hedging came in fashion,
The March of Progress gave my realm
Enclosure and Plantation.
'Twas then, to soothe their discontent,
I showed each pounded Master,
However fast the Commons went,
I went a little faster!

When Pigg and Jorrocks held the stage,
And Steam had linked the Shires,
I broke the staid Victorian age
To posts, and rails, and wires.
Then fifty mile was none too far
To go by train to cover,
Till some dam' sutler pupped a Car,
And decent sport was over!

When men grew shy of hunting stag
For fear the Law might try 'em,
The car put up an average bag
Of twenty dead per diem.
Then every road was made a rink
For Coroners to sit on;
And so began, in skid and stink,
The real blood-sports of Britain!

Rudyard Kipling, O.M.

The Bean

My dear old Bean has gone to the Happy Hunting Ground,
after carrying a huntsman for the last eight years of his life.
I shall never see his like again.

Of all the gallant sportsmen that ever I have seen,
The best and quite the gamest was my good old horse The Bean.
The days we've had together no tongue may ever tell;
Three counties knew the worth of him, and wished the old horse well.
From Hereford to Shrewsbury town they one and all enquire,
"How goes it with the chestnut horse – the one that jumps the wire?"

They knew him in Kilkenny, he's famous up at Bree,
Where Wexford's double banks stretch out towards the sea.
The Irish thrusters shook their heads, for "He won't do," they said:
"You cannot cross the Irish banks on a horse that's English bred;"
And though they tried their hardest you showed them all the way
From the cubbing in September till we finished up in May.
You swam across the river when the day had got so late
That the car turned on the headlights to let you jump the gate.
They talk of you in Wexford still, the land of bog and gorse;
'Twill be long ere they forget you, my gallant chestnut horse.
They tell of you from Ticklerton right on to Offa's Dyke,
And along the wild Welsh border they have never seen your like;
They saw you going at your ease, no matter how they ride;
Come what may throughout the day you never turned aside.
So when the long last day is done, and life's last covert's drawn;
When Gabriel turns his phantom steed and sadly sounds his horn;
There's just one thing I'll ask of Fate –
And that's for my chestnut horse to wait
To carry me over the Golden Gate
On Resurrection morn.

Dalesman

WE HAVE NO WISH TO EXAGGERATE

We have no wish to exaggerate
The worth of the Sports we prize,
Some toil for their Church, and some for their State,
And some for their Merchandise;
Some traffic and trade in the city's mart,
Some travel by land and sea,
Some follow science, some cleave to art,
And some to scandal and tea;
And some for their country and their Queen
Would fight, if a chance they had.
Good sooth, 'twere a sorry world, I ween,
If we all went galloping mad;
Yet if once we efface the joys of the chase
From the land, and outroot the stud,
Goodbye to the Anglo-Saxon Race!
Farewell to the Norman Blood!

Adam Lindsay Gordon

RED RUM

The only horse to win the Grand National three times – 1973, 1974 and 1977

It's said there are horses for courses,
Red Rum makes this point very clear;
Three *firsts* and a couple of seconds –
His astonishing Aintree career!

Forbidding, formidable fences
Four miles and a half of the track;
Red Rum, all alert in his senses,
Is in tune with the man on his back.

Around forty magnificent chasers
Well prepared by their trainers' skilled art
For this greatest of all steeplechases
Fit and ready and rearing to start.

"They are off" with high hearts and high courage;
"Every horse has the National won!"
But few there will be at the finish
For there's gruelling work to be done.

His wonderful galloping quarters
Land him easily over The Chair;
Spring-heeled and well balanced at Becher's
He flies like a bird through the air.

While his rivals are falling about him
He cocks an intelligent ear,
He knows he must keep out of trouble
And there's plenty of that around here.

The last fence, and then the long run in,
Sustained by his courage alone,
Till he hears the crowd roaring for 'Rummy'
And knows he's triumphantly home.

And now he is fêted and honoured
Befitting so gallant a horse.
His statue at Aintree proclaims him
King of the National Course.

Mary Vaughan – 1988

A bronze statue of Red Rum was unveiled by the Princess Royal during the Grand National meeting at Aintree in March 1988; and Red Rum paraded on the course.

For Dawn Run And Jonjo O'Neill

She came over to do something
Never done before;
She'd won the Champion Hurdle in 1984
And now she thought the Gold Cup might be added to her score.

Right from the start she dictated the race
And took them along at a blistering pace,
She made jumping mistakes – never mind when or where –
But they cost her some lengths that were not going spare.

She was third at the last and I feared she was done,
But that seems a word quite unknown to Dawn Run.
As they breasted the hill Wayward Lad had the lead
With Forgive 'n' Forget showing wonderful speed.

Sure of her courage Jonjo asked for *all*
And the crowd held its breath as she answered his call.
Up the Cheltenham hill ever lengthening her stride
Measured and strong as an incoming tide.

When she caught them, and passed them, there rose such a roar
That even *this* racecourse had not heard before.
Wild cheers from the crowd and hats in the air
Acclaimed a length's win for this game Irish mare.

There were no 'hard luck' tales in this race bravely won
When history was made by Jonjo and Dawn Run.

Mary Vaughan
Cheltenham, 13th March 1986

LESTER PIGGOTT IS GOING TO GAOL

The greatest jockey of all times
In gaol for tax evasion crimes.

He was the housewife's 'Golden Boy',
The tipsters special pride and joy;
When Lester gets astride a horse
The punters up and down the course
Rely upon his special skill
And place their money for a kill,
An almost perfect judge of pace
With bum in air he'll win the race.
He'd ridden for the rich and great
And sometimes for the Head of State.
He'd thrilled the crowds on Epsom Down
Nine Derbys gained unique renown.
Nine Derbys! – do I make it clear?
He was a horseman without peer –
And now the Law has brought him low
Oh! Lester how can this be so?

He only understood race courses
And riding winners on great horses.

Mary Vaughan 1988

ARKLE

Few words are needed Arkle to acclaim
The greatest of great horses of his time.
Named for a Scottish Mountain he became
A legend, as enduring, as sublime.

Mary Vaughan, 1986